VALUE MIX

by

Guerric de Ternay

Your Audience

Your Proposition

Worldviews

Customer Exp.

Positioning

Goals

+

Concerns

User Exp.

Features + Benefits

Context

Alternatives

The Value Mix by Guerric de Ternay

Copyright © 2018-2021 Guerric de Ternay

Author name: Guerric de Ternay

Title: The Value Mix: Create Meaningful Products and Services for Your Audience

For those who shake up things,

challenge the status quo, and make

cool stuff happen.

TABLE OF CONTENTS

ACKNOWLEDGEMENTS

A massive thank you to Ségolène and Amaury for always helping me with everything I do!

Big big thanks to María, Manu, Oskar, Patricia, Alex, Kirsten, Olli, and Toby for their constant support and the endless crazy chats about life, creativity, and innovation!

NEW EDITION

The Value Mix was first published in 2018 on Leanpub and in 2019 on Amazon. A few years later, I still believe that the framework presented in the book can significantly help businesses create value for their audience by launching bolder, more meaningful propositions.

I wanted to update the content to add more examples, clarify some explanations, and prompt you to action with the "key questions" you'll find at the end of each chapter.

Throughout the book, I refer to "you" as the person responsible for marketing and innovation in the company. But over the years, I realised that many readers are also consultants, students, and investors. This shows how universal the topic of creating new value propositions is.

I hope you enjoy this new edition of the book.

INTRODUCTION

It's difficult to create a product that people really want to buy and use. There's no silver bullet to success. It's hard work because there's lots of uncertainty.

Those who do this for a living know that.

Fortunately, over the past two decades, the management literature has equipped us with better ways to create new products, such as:

1. **Customer centricity.** *Design thinking* and *customer development* are two approaches that encourage us to build products for potential customers rather than trying to find customers for new products;

2. **Iterative development.** The *lean startup* methodology pushes us to apply the scientific method and pursue continuous learning and product iteration to create better products.

But, we are still missing a way to organise the information and insight we gather about our customers to clearly define what they need and want.

To help you develop successful products and services, you need a framework that:

1. Allows you to gain a deep understanding of what value means for your customers;
2. Gives you a shared language to align with your team on a strategy for the new products and services that you will launch.

This framework must be as accurate as possible, by capturing enough nuances to reflect the reality of our world. But it also needs to be practical enough so it can be used by anyone in your company who is involved in the process of launching new products and services.

Going beyond a limiting framework

Under the pressure of growth and profit targets, most organisations focus too much on their commercial priorities and not enough on creating value for their customers and users.

Putting the people who buy and use your products and services at the centre of your new product development process sounds common sense. But this isn't an intuitive behaviour. It seems that it's easier for a company to be product-centric than human-centred.

The easy way to force a business to focus on their customers and users is to talk about "finding a solution to a problem", i.e., your customers have *problems* and your product is the *solution*.

This framework, which comes from the world of engineering, does help. But it creates the limiting belief that innovation is about "finding a solution to a problem". The "problem-solution" dichotomy works. But it doesn't capture enough nuances. This framework limits the scope of value creation. It misses the fact that people do not just buy a solution. They also buy brands, stories, emotional benefits, and experiences.

Solving a problem isn't the only way to create value for your customers. What people perceive as value isn't just functional. It also relies on how your products and services make them feel.

Innocent, a smoothie brand, didn't create value for its customers by solving a "smoothie" problem. The company created stories and remarkable experiences that made people feel connected to the Innocent brand.

Marshall, a brand known for its music amplifiers, didn't solve a "headphones" problem when it launched a range of branded headphones. The brand built on its heritage of music amplifiers, creating value by making its customers dream and feel like they were at a concert watching their favourite band.

How to make the most of reading these pages

"Action is what produces results. Knowledge is only potential power until it comes into the hands of someone who knows how to get himself to take effective action."

— TONY ROBBINS, Life strategist

The Value Mix aims to make it easier for you to think about the nuances of creating products and services that people will want, i.e., creating value for them.

I wanted this framework to be simple to remember and easy to use, while still acknowledging the complexity and nuances of the real world.

Together, we will go through each element of the Value Mix. You'll get everything you need to understand the concept of value creation and then turn what you learnt into action.

Let me emphasise that this isn't a box-filling exercise.

Reality is complex. So one cannot pretend to capture in a single framework all the nuances necessary to create successful products and services.

This book aims to guide your thinking. The real value lies in doing the work, i.e., understanding your customers at a deeper emotional level and developing new ways to create value for them.

I would call it a success if the Value Mix inspires you to approach more effectively how you research your market and how you build new products and services.

The ultimate objective: creating value for your customers by building the products and services that matter to them.

The inception of the Value Mix

"Creativity is just connecting things. When you ask creative people how they did something, they feel a little guilty because they didn't really do it, they just saw something."

– STEVE JOBS, Founder of Apple

New ideas come from finding connections among the things we've experienced, heard, read, and observed.

This is how I got the idea for the Value Mix.

The ideas in this book come from connecting many things: my journey building my own businesses, my experience running innovation projects for Fortune 500 companies, chats with fellow entrepreneurs and investors, and the writing of many businesspeople.

These ideas also connect multiple disciplines, such as economics, design, psychology, copywriting, strategy, software development, and marketing.

The result:

We are lucky as we live in an ocean of nearly free information. The difficulty is to make this knowledge practical so it can help us be more creative and make better decisions.

The value of this book comes from turning the elements related to creating new products and services into a logical framework. It will help you as you build a new business, innovate in an established organisation, or invest in startups.

PART I
CREATING VALUE

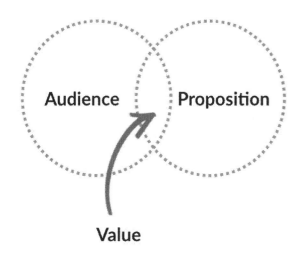

The imperative of value creation

"The value is in what gets used, not in what gets built."

– KRIS GALE, Founder of Clover Health

Your business can only succeed if it creates and sells products and services that your audience will want to buy and use—a meaningful proposition.

What's clear is that your audience will want what you sell only if they believe that it creates for them more value than something else they could buy and use.

So how do you make sure you create value? What are the elements that can help you understand your audience? And what are the things you need to consider to create the right proposition?

Audience: Those you serve

The left side of the framework represents the **audience**, i.e., the people who will buy and use your products and services.

It includes three elements that help you segment your market by answering the following questions:

- What are their beliefs?
- What are they trying to achieve?
- What would prevent them from choosing your proposition?

This side of the framework aims to help you identify what creates value for your audience.

Proposition: What you offer

The right side of the Value Mix framework is about your proposition, i.e., what you offer to create value in the lives of your customers and users.

There are a number of elements you can play with to design a proposition that feels meaningful and relevant.

It's is not just about the functionalities of a product or a service. It's about the overall experience you create for your audience.

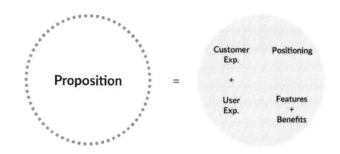

As a proposition, the iPhone isn't just a high-end smartphone. It's also about how you experience the interoperability with the AppStore, the AirPods, iCloud, Apple TV, Safari, Apple Wallet, and the MacBook.

Landscape: When your audience and proposition interact

Your **audience** and your **proposition** do not live in a vacuum. In the real world:

- Your audience lives in a specific **context**. They are in an environment and experience situations that influence what they do and how they think.
- Your proposition is constantly compared to **alternatives**. When someone in your target audience considers buying your product, they often have a set of other alternatives in mind.

Having clarity on the context of your audience's life and the set of alternatives that are available to them is decisive in creating a proposition that is relevant and meaningful for your audience.

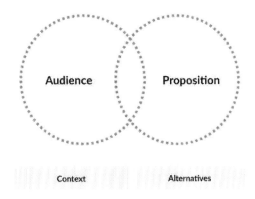

Context   Alternatives

PART II
UNDERSTANDING YOUR AUDIENCE

Chapter 1:

Your Audience

"The purpose of business is to create and keep a customer."

– Peter Drucker, Management consultant

To create meaningful propositions, you must understand what can create value for your audience. You have to be clear on why they need you in their lives.

Leading brands are *audience-informed* (2) but they are *vision-led* (1).

1. It's your role to set the vision and create propositions that your audience will want but never think to ask.
2. But to create something they want, you need to understand your market. You need to have clear answers to: Who is it for? Why will they get it?

As you try to understand your audience at a deeper level to identify what they need and want, there are four things that you should especially focus on:

- **Context** - The context is the surrounding that influences what your audience needs and wants to achieve—their goals.
- **Goals** - In the pursuit of goals, your audience will buy and use products and services that help them achieve the progress and outcomes they envision.
- **Worldviews** - To choose which products and services to buy and use, they rely on their worldviews, which are the beliefs, biases, and opinions they hold about the world.
- **Concerns** - They also interrogate their concerns about what they are about to buy. These are all the reasons and feelings that are holding them back from buying your proposition (or an alternative one).

Chapter 2:

Context

They know what you need

A few years ago, I visited Milan over the summer. There were a lot of hawkers selling things in the street.

Here's what I noticed:

On a beautiful sunny day, they would sell sunglasses and cold water. But if it started raining, you would see them immediately selling umbrellas and waterproof ponchos.

These street hawkers understood how context influences what people want.

Context: Definition

Context includes time, location, situations, people, weather, events, and all the surrounding that trigger the need or desire to achieve a goal.

Context is a **link of causality**. It causes someone to want to do something. Knowing what the **triggers** are will help you to identify what your audience needs or wants to achieve and why.

For example, a nutritionist must understand the events and situations that trigger a need or desire to change one's diet. Is it a New Year's resolution? Is it because of a wedding? Is it related to a health issue? Knowing the context will help the nutritionist reach her clients at the right time and offer the right approach.

Correlation is not causality

It's Thursday night. Here's Jake, a 27-year-old who works as a senior designer for a tech company in New York.

Can you guess what happens next? Probably not…

Knowing that Jake is a male who is 27 and works in design for a tech company doesn't tell us why on a Thursday night he got takeaway pizzas and why on another night he went to a trendy cocktail bar.

Attributes don't tell us much about what people do. They may correlate with some behaviours. But they do not cause them.

Context is the trigger. It gives you more insight into what people want to achieve.

Maybe Jake got pizzas because he had friends coming over to play poker. The context of playing poker with his friends triggered the desire and need to get some food. As its convenient, cheap, and yummy, pizzas seemed a good option.

A tool: Why create a customer journey

To understand the context your audience lives in, you have to put yourself in their shoes.

- What is the context of the purchase?
- What has triggered their decision?
- And what is the context of use?

Building a **customer journey** helps gain clarity on all the steps that led someone to buy a product or service and to use it.

It is a great tool to create a proposition that truly helps your audience achieve their goals. But it's also helpful to define how, when, and where your proposition must show up in their lives.

A customer journey is a **visual guide**—not the truth. It helps visualise what is happening in the real world. The complexity and variety of customer journeys cannot be modelled accurately.

That being said, even a rough customer journey will help you understand your audience at a deeper level.

By mapping the customer journeys of your audience, you will better understand what triggers specific needs and desires. It will help you create more relevant propositions, and also allow you to identify the best moment and channels to reach them.

Think again about the example of the nutritionist. If the nutritionist understands that most brides start thinking about a new diet when they try wedding dresses, she could partner with brands to offer tailored nutrition plan for the future brides and advertise them in stores, in wedding magazines, and on Pinterest by targeting keywords related to getting married.

A tool: How to create a customer journey

First, choose who in your audience you want to focus on.

Then, map the key moments of the journey. An easy way to start is to use the five following steps: (1) Awareness, (2) Consideration, (3) Purchase, (4) Use (or Consumption), and (5) Referral.

To build the journey, you pick two steps and you ask yourself: "What happens in between?". And you keep doing this—picking two steps and breaking down what happens in between—until you get to a satisfying level of nuance and granularity.

For each step, you must find out what your audience is doing (*actions*), struggling with (*frustrations*), and wishing (*aspirations*).

Depending on your level of knowledge of your audience, you may need to do additional research to have a clearer view of what happens at each step.

Stage	Aware	Consider	Purchase	Use	Refer
Doing					
Struggling with					
Wishing					

Example format for a customer journey

Key questions about your audience

Here are some questions that can guide the way you generate customer insight:

When your audience is in a particular context:

- What are they trying to achieve (*goals*)?
- What are the beliefs that influence what they're trying to do (*worldviews*)?
- What could prevent them from doing this with your proposition (*concerns*)?

Let's now dig into each question.

Chapter 3:

Goals

A new job. But why?

Miranda (not her real name) was working as a cashier in a supermarket. She liked the company but her schedule didn't suit her family life. She would be off when her son was in school and would often have to work quite late in the evening.

But recently, one of her friends started working as a software developer for a startup. It pays well, apparently. So Miranda saw coding as an opportunity to get a better job. She wanted to be there for her family.

Miranda started using Codecademy, a learning platform. She would study and do the exercises before and after work, even during her lunch breaks to finish the course so that she could move out of retail and do something interesting that would suit better her family life.

Let's dig into the details:

Here Miranda wasn't pleased with her current job because the schedule didn't suit her family life (*context*).

She decided that she'd like to get a job as a developer to be able to spend more time with her family (*goal*).

So she started taking online classes on Codecademy (*proposition*) to learn about coding and get a job she will like more (*achieved goal*).

Goals: Definition

"People don't want to buy a quarter-inch drill. They want a quarter-inch hole!"

– THEODORE LEVITT, Professor at Harvard Business School

A **goal** is the outcome or progress your target audience needs or wants to achieve in a particular context.

Context and goals go together.

The context triggers the goals that lead to buying and using a product or a service.

Focusing on the goals of your target audience helps you spot what causes them to buy and use your proposition or an alternative one.

When the owner of a small e-commerce website is planning the marketing strategy of her business (*context*), she wants to be able to analyse the performance of previous marketing campaigns (*goal*). This causes her to use Google Analytics (*proposition*).

Here are two ways to link context and goals together:

- When … (*context*), I want to … (*goal*) by using … (*proposition*).
- Here is where I am today (*current context*). And here is where I want your product or service (*proposition*) to take me (*achieved goal*).

What to do with this: Segment the market accurately

"Your most unhappy customers are your greatest source of learning."

— *BILL GATES, ex-CEO of Microsoft*

You can use goals to identify different segments in the market. Once you know precisely what they want to achieve, you can create propositions that are more relevant in the way they help each segment.

Most of the time, a proposition didn't satisfy a customer because it didn't help them achieve their goals. It didn't match their expectations.

For example, someone in Ireland buys a nice coat for the mid-season. But it happens that the coat is just water-resistant, it's not fully waterproof. So after a heavy rain, the customer is disappointed. He thought he had a nice coat for commuting to work. Now, he realised he can't wear it when it rains.

Identifying the specific goals of each segment will help you make sure that you can address their needs and desires in the most relevant ways, and articulate well how you position your proposition.

Goal-based segmentation often shows up in the pricing strategy of a business.

Airlines master the art of goal-based segmentation, even giving names to the different tiers based on what the segment of the audience is trying to achieve:

- Economy class is designed for those who want to go from A to B as cheaply as possible.

- Business class is designed for those who are going from A to B and want to be in the right conditions to be able to work before, during, and after the flight.

What to do with this: Build the right proposition

"The customer rarely buys what the business thinks it sells him."

– PETER DRUCKER, Management consultant

Helping your audience achieve their goals in the most effective and efficient way is at the core of creating value for them.

So being clear on the goals of your target audience makes a big difference. Once you really understand what they want to achieve, it makes building the right proposition so much easier, because you now know what to focus on.

Spotify transformed the way we listen to music. Its product team has been focused on helping users achieve their goals around listening to music, making the experience so much better than buying and using CDs. For that, the company created new features such as:

- A Friend feed (*feature*), when you want to share the music you like with your friends and what music they listen to (*goal*);

- Sport playlists (*feature*), when you want to motivate yourself with some music when you go running (*goal*);

- Spotify Discover (*feature*), when you need new ideas of music to listen to (*goal*).

Goals are the foundation on which you can build the features and customer experience that will be most helpful to your audience.

What to do with this: Find new opportunities

"People don't like to be sold but they love to buy."

– JEFFREY GITOMER, Sales consultant

When we define the goals of an audience, it's tempting to focus more on the functional aspect of their goals, e.g., "When I travel for work, I need to have a small suitcase that is allowed in the cabin".

A company that identifies that goal will inevitably have a narrow focus on selling suitcases that can be accepted in the cabin.

But if you dig deeper into the emotional aspect by asking "why?", you may realise that it may be about the speed of boarding, but it's also about safety, i.e., "When I travel for work, I need a small suitcase that guarantees that I can have with me in the cabin, because I want to know that my stuff is safe."

Here's the interesting insight coming out!

The second expression of the goal allows many more possibilities to help your audience. Now, it's not just about making a compact suitcase. It's also about making a suitcase that will reassure them that no one will be able to open it. You want to make your audience feel that when they put their belongings in the suitcase, it's almost as safe as putting them in a safe deposit box.

By reframing the goals and really digging into the emotional aspect, you may uncover interesting insight that will spark new ideas on how you can best serve your audience.

A tool: Customer interviews

As you saw in the example above, interviewing your customers can help you uncover useful bits of insight that will then allow you to create more value for them.

But for this, you need to ask good questions.

You should avoid asking conditional questions using "would". These lead to vague or generic answers about what someone would do in a hypothetical situation.

Instead, ask for stories. Ask questions about what someone did in the past.

Try to get as much detail as possible to really understand what they did and how they felt. And then, politely dig into the reasons they did these things, or felt that way by asking them "why?". Don't hesitate to ask "why?" several times. You often get the best insight after the second or third "why".

Here's an example about going to the gym: When I ask someone: "Do you go to the gym?" They often tell me: "Yes. I go 3-4 times a week." But then, if I ask: "What about last week? Did you go to the gym?" The usual answer is: "Hmmm. No. But that's different. I didn't go because…"

A generic claim isn't as good as a specific story.

Bad questions are generic or conditional: Do you ever do…? Do you think you would…? If [conditional event], would you…?

Better questions are specific and about the past: What did you do? When did you…? Where? With whom? Why did you decide to do this? How did you feel? Tell me more about that. Why did you feel that way?

A key question about your audience:

What goals are you helping your audience to achieve?

Chapter 4:

Worldviews

What makes them cool?

When the summer comes (*context*), we start wearing sunglasses to protect our eyes (*functional goal*) and look cool (*emotional goal*).

This is the case for Peter and Alex who both live in Paris. Both of them have similar goals when it gets sunny: "to protect their eyes and to look cool".

But then, how can we explain that Peter wears a classic pair of Ray-Ban, while Alex has a pair he bought from a startup brand called Jimmy Fairly?

They aren't interested in the same stories.

Let's dig into the details:

Peter and Alex share similar goals. But they have different worldviews, i.e., different sets of values, beliefs, biases, and opinions.

They both relied (unconsciously) on their own worldviews to guide their choice of sunglasses.

- Peter felt reassured about Ray-Ban. It's a well-known brand and most people would approve his choice.
- Alex wanted something more social and less mainstream. He values that Jimmy Fairly gives a pair of glasses to someone in need when he buys his own pair of stylish glasses. And he likes that not that many people actually know about the brand.

Worldviews: Definition

"A worldview is not who you are. It's what you believe. It's your biases. A worldview is not forever. It's what the consumer believes right now."

– SETH GODIN, AUTHOR OF ALL MARKETERS ARE LIARS

The context tells you why and when some specific goals arise in your customers' lives. And the goals tell you what they are trying to achieve. But context and goals cannot tell us why someone chooses a brand over another one.

This is what worldviews help you do.

Worldviews are a set of beliefs, values, taste, attitudes, and opinions that your audience relies on when they make decisions.

A worldview is subjective. It's a personal preference that is based on what someone believes to be true.

You can think of worldviews as a way of seeing and judging things. They are the lenses through which your audience looks at the world when they are trying to achieve their goals. Worldviews guide your audience's actions and influence their choices.

Why does someone decide to buy a $450 Dyson vacuum cleaner, while someone else goes for a Eureka vacuum cleaner, which is labelled as the Amazon's First Choice and costs only $69?

Maybe it's a difference in disposable income. Or maybe it's that the former customer loves well-designed products, and the latter believes it's good to be frugal.

Dyson tells the "design" story well. And Eureka positioned itself to speak the language of frugality showing good value for money.

What to do with this: A segmentation tool

"Segments must be Measurable, Substantial, Accessible, Differentiable, and Actionable."

— PHILIP KOTLER, Professor at the Kellogg School of Management

Worldviews are useful criteria for **segmenting** your market. What people believe to be true can help you predict their decisions more accurately than their age or their job.

Looking at worldviews gives you the nuances that you miss when you only search for "customer problems". It tells you at a deeper level why someone chooses an alternative versus another.

Young parents face many challenges. On the weekend (*context*), one of their problems is: "How can we have a nice family time and make our children happy?" (*goal*).

For some parents, McDonald's means Happy Meal, Big Mac, nostalgia, and nice moments with their children (*worldview*). For other parents, McDonald's means junk food, saturated fat, and too much carb. It's something they don't want their children to have (*worldview*).

Of course, this is a simplified view of the market. But here's the question: If you were running McDonald's, would you try to please both worldviews?

What to do with this: A storytelling tool

"Great brands are the ones that tell the best stories. Sure, good products and service matter, but stories are what connect people with companies."

— *JASON FRIED, CEO of Basecamp*

Telling stories is key to building a strong brand. Stories are what make a product stand out in front of your audience. Meaningful propositions don't just solve a functional problem; they create an emotional connection between your brand and your audience.

Stories help you affirm why your product or service exists. It tells your customers how your proposition creates.

A common model of story is the "before and after" story. Describe their lives before your proposition was part of their day-to-day. Then, tell the story of how your proposition can transform their lives and what outcome it can help them achieve.

If you want to get someone excited about signing up for your upcoming online course, you don't spend hours explaining the outline of the course. You tell them about how this course can transform their personal or professional lives, i.e., what value it creates for them. A compelling way to do so is to tell them the story of their lives after they've taken the course.

The ad of an online course about yoga may tell you about how you will never have your terrible back pain anymore or how a daily yoga session will keep you energised throughout the day.

Good stories reinforce the existing worldviews of your audience. They don't try to get them to change their mind.

In the example above, the yoga course reinforces the belief that having the right level of physical activity can help alleviate back pain or make you feel more energetic.

Ways of telling stories

Storytelling is not just about copywriting and advertising.

The smell of a French bakery tells the story of "fresh bread". The cocktail offered at a nail salon tells the story of "pampering".

You build a story through every aspect of the customer experience.

In 2011, I created GoudronBlanc, a brand that makes elegant T-shirts that men love. A worldview I spotted was that more and more men wear T-shirts instead of suits when they are at work.

To tell the story of what I call "T-shirt is the new suit", I took photos of famous French entrepreneurs wearing GoudronBlanc T-shirts in their office. The story was even covered by a national newspaper.

As said before, a good story is anchored in existing beliefs. It confirms your audience's biases. It plays on their perception.

But the story has to be true. If your proposition cannot deliver on what you're promising, it won't work.

Evaluating worldviews

"Marketing succeeds when enough people with similar worldviews come together in a way that allows marketers to reach them cost-effectively."

— SETH GODIN, Author of All Marketers Are Liars

Now, you understand how worldviews play a significant role in how your audience assesses value and makes choices.

Worldviews are subjective. They are based on personal experiences, on what others say, on how the world reacts to what one does.

Most worldviews are personal. But some worldviews are shared.

To build successful propositions, you want to address worldviews that are shared by a group of people. When people have a common worldview, they talk about it. They talk about the products and services that relate to that worldview.

And this will make it easier for your ideas and stories to spread at an affordable cost, through word of mouth.

Professionals who value their time highly will always be keen on telling others about their productivity system. If there's a new app they find exciting, they will blog about it, share it on social media, and may even share YouTube videos about how to use it.

Chocolate lovers, who believe that industrial chocolate isn't worth a penny, will be super enthusiastic with the idea of telling their friends about a new artisanal chocolate brand.

How to spot worldviews

Identifying worldviews is about spotting patterns. It's the difficult work of the innovator, the market researcher, the product manager, or the investor.

There isn't a magic way of doing it. But some things can help you find evidence that a worldview exists:

-   **Social Listening**: Browse forums, Reddit, Facebook groups, YouTube videos, blog articles. What are some of the most viral articles and videos? What do people tell each other on social media?
-   **Customer Interviews:** Interview people who share a hobby, have similar lifestyles, etc. What do they believe strongly? Have they recently started doing something new?

When doing social listening and customer interviews, it's worth paying extra attention to a few things, such as:

-   **Influencers** — Who are the people who seem to lead and spread the worldview?

- **Books they read** — What are the books they read and recommend?
- **Videos they watch** — What are the movies, documentaries, and YouTube videos they watch and recommend?
- **Places they go to** — Where can you find them? Are there specific online platforms where they hang out?
- **Brands they use** — What are other brands they buy and talk about? Why these?

Example: The digital nomad worldview

Who they are:

Digital nomads are a community of people who work remotely to live nomadic lives. They often take advantage of not having to be in an office to travel and live in foreign countries.

The evidence they exist:

- **What they read**: 4-Hour Workweek, Vagabonding
- **Influencers**: Matt Mullenweg, Tim Ferriss
- **Where they hang out**: nomadlist.com, reddit.com/r/digitalnomad/, coworking spaces, coffee shops…
- **Brands they use**: Cocoon (cable organiser), Qwstion (backpack), Revolut (banking)

What they say and believe:

- "I'm young. Why should I be trapped in a life that isn't for me?"
- "The corporate world is boring."
- "If I can do it remotely, why should I commute to an office?"

- "Have you been in Asia? There are so many cool things to explore."
- "Why should I live in an expensive American city, when I can have a much better life abroad?"

A key question about your audience:

What shared worldviews are you addressing?

Chapter 5:

Concerns

In search of the perfect travel companion

I have some back issues. This can turn a long haul flight into a nightmare.

In April 2018, I had 5 long haul flights booked to travel for work and leisure (*context*). As I wanted to avoid suffering from lower back pain while travelling (*goal*), I started searching for the perfect travel pillow (*proposition*).

After a few Google searches, I short-listed five brands. All seemed to do the job. But then, I started asking myself:

- Is it going to be firm enough to hold my head?
- Is the pillow going to lose its shape if I fold it into my bag?
- What about the fabric, is it going to be comfortable or make my skin itchy?

All of these questions are concerns.

They can be dangerous for a brand, as they can stop a prospect from buying.

The brand that ultimately won my purchase is the one that created the most certainty. It answered all of my questions and reassured me that I was buying a good travel pillow.

Concerns: Definition

"There is only one boss. The customer. And he can fire everybody in the company from the chairman on down, simply by spending his money somewhere else."

— SAM WALTON, FOUNDER OF WALMART

Concerns are all the arguments (*logical reasons*) and feelings (*emotional reasons*) that prevent your target customers from buying your proposition or an alternative one.

When we think about concerns, we often consider "price" first.

But concerns are not just about price-sensitivity. They also include the "learning curve", "switching cost", lack of social proof, lack of clarity on how it works, the pricing model, questions about durability, or a new version of your product that is coming soon.

The level of concerns depends on the context and what your audience wants to achieve.

The concerns about buying a new smartphone are more important than the concerns about trying a new brand of Greek yoghurt.

In B to B, the concerns about contracting for a new cloud service are more significant than the concerns about choosing the food provider for a company event. This will often translate into the number of people involved in making the decision.

It's always a "logical" concern

The concerns of your audience come from the potential negative consequences that they want to avoid when they buy and use your proposition.

- I ordered this new flavoured tea, but I don't like the taste.
- I bought these shoes online, but they don't fit me.
- I subscribed to a fashion magazine, but the content isn't as good as I expected.
- I signed up to a CRM tool, but there are lots of hidden costs.

These are all "logical" stories that your potential customers are telling themselves. Some may be objective, others may be more subjective.

I put logical in quotation marks to emphasise the following point: these stories are logical to them. You may think: "It's crazy to worry about this". But what matters is what's in their minds, not what's in yours.

Anticipating concerns when you create your proposition makes it easier to sell it later. It's about designing the customer experience to answer the questions from the voice that is in the head of your audience.

You want your proposition to reassure them that they are making the right decision.

Certainty plays a big role

When you sell a product or a service, you sell *certainty*.

You sell:

- the certainty that it's the best offer available,
- the certainty that they are making the right decision,
- the certainty that it's going to work as they expect,
- the certainty that their friends will like it,
- the certainty that the boss will be happy, etc.

Concerns arise when your audience feels that there's a lack of certainty.

This is why good marketers focus on building trust with their target audience. The more trustworthy you appear, the easier it is for your audience to buy.

Free trial, freemium, referral, affiliate, user-generated content, etc. These are many features you can bake into the customer experience to increase certainty (and reduce concerns) when your audience is considering buying your proposition.

A key question about your audience:

What will hold people back from buying your proposition?

PART III
SHAPING YOUR
PROPOSITION

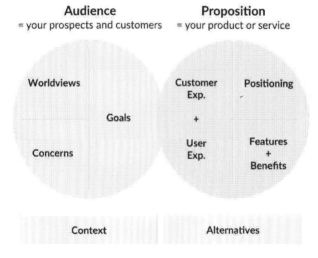

Chapter 6:

Your proposition

"Ideas don't come out fully formed. They only become clear as you work on them. You just have to get started."

— MARK Zuckerberg, CEO of Facebook

It's quite easy to come up with new product ideas. A typical ideation workshop can lead to a hundred or more ideas.

What's more difficult is to turn these ideas into fully-fledged propositions.

The lack of detail about a proposition can become a barrier to implementing it. You need to be clear on the detail to align with your team. You must be able to articulate your proposition to make a business case for investing in testing it and implementing it.

You need clarity on the detail to be able to test your proposition with potential customers by following the *lean startup* or *design thinking* methodology.

The **proposition** comes after the audience in the book because a proposition is something you build *for* an audience. It's about making something for your audience, instead of trying to find customers for what you made.

To create value for your audience, you must understand them first. Then, once you understand the context, their goals, their worldviews, and their concerns, it'll be easier to create propositions that are right for them.

In this section, I explore the six elements that you must consider to build a coherent proposition. The objective is to give you and your team a shared language to work on creating meaningful propositions.

I'll focus on the following:

- **Alternatives** – Alternatives are the benchmarks you can use to make sure you build a relevant proposition.
- **Features and Benefits** – While benefits are about helping your audience achieve their goals, features help you describe and prioritise what needs to be built.
- **Positioning** – Your positioning is how you'd like your audience to perceive your proposition and

what you want them to remember and tell their friends about it.

- **CX and UX** – The customer experience (CX) and user experience (UX) are the ways your proposition shows up in the lives of your customers (and users).

Chapter 7:

Alternatives

The best way to travel

When I was studying in London, the holiday period (*context*) was the perfect moment to go to Paris to visit my parents (*goal*).

I had several options: train, coach, airplane, or getting someone to drive me there.

As a student, I had time but no money (*worldview*), so the Eurostar, the fastest way to get there, wasn't my only alternative.

Every time I would go to Paris, I was balancing price, comfort, and the speed to choose how to get there.

Eurostar is a railway service. Ouibus, Eurolines, and Megabus are in the bus industry. Air France and Ryan Air are airlines. BlaBlaCar is in an online marketplace.

But every time I wanted to go to Paris, they were all competing for my pennies.

They are all alternatives to one another.

Alternatives: Definition

Alternatives are propositions that your audience perceives as comparable, since they can also help them achieve their goals.

Once they bought an alternative, they become less interested in having the other alternative propositions. It's what economists call the "law of diminishing marginal utility". If you just bought a new smartphone, you're less interested in having another one.

Businesses usually look at competitive propositions in their category, i.e., direct competitors.

But it is more accurate to look at the competitive landscape from the eyes of your audience, comparing goal-based alternatives.

Example:

Who is the biggest competitor of Coca-Cola (the soda)?

- Pepsi? Red Bull?
- Fruit juices? Smoothies?
- Wine? Beer?

- Coffee? Tea?
- Water?

Unintended consequences

"The reason [the railroads] defined their industry incorrectly was that they were railroad oriented instead of transportation oriented. They were product-oriented instead of customer-oriented."

– THEODORE LEVITT, Professor at Harvard Business School

The issue with only considering direct competitors instead of a broader set of alternatives is that a company may tend to focus on the features of its proposition, not on what its audience is trying to achieve.

The company ends up in an arms race trying to offer better features and functionalities than its direct competitors. But they miss the point because they are not looking at the world in the way their audience does.

The direct competitor of a DSLR camera is another DSLR camera. But when someone wants to take photos, they may also consider other alternatives such as a smartphone, a disposable camera, a Polaroid, or a GoPro. That's because they are looking for the best way to achieve their goals, which also fits with their worldview. They are not limiting themselves to a product category.

It's important to look at your market from the point of view of your audience.

Knowing what your audience considers as alternatives gives useful information on their goals, their worldviews, and therefore what's important for them when they make their choice.

It's a good source of insight to build a more relevant proposition. It gives you the material to build a story and position your proposition in a way that speaks to your audience and makes it stand out against the other alternatives.

A tool: Alternatives mapping

An **alternatives map** is a tool that helps visualise how your audience thinks about your proposition compared to relevant alternatives.

It helps you gain clarity on their decision-making process:

- What criteria matter to them?
- How do alternatives compare to each other?
- What alternative performs the best?

Understanding how your audience chooses the best option for them will help you better design a proposition that will create more value for them.

Here are the steps necessary to build an alternatives map:

1. Identify the range of alternatives that your audience is likely to compare with one another;
2. Lay out the criteria they use to make their decisions of buying one over another;
3. Rank how each alternative performs for each criterion.

Here's an example of an alternatives map for someone who wants to go from London to Paris:

Alternatives for going from London to Paris

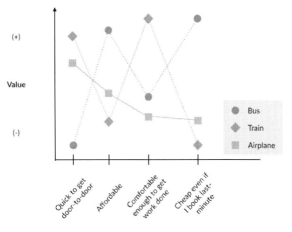

Attributes that matter to your audience

It's clear that the train is the fastest and most comfortable alternative. Going by bus is the most affordable and flexible option. Flying to Paris is somewhat in between.

A key question about your proposition:

What alternatives does your target audience have in mind when they consider your proposition?

Chapter 8:

Feature + Benefits

The one who wanted to show off

I'll never forget this scene from Friends:

Chandler opens a bulky laptop, which is typical of the 90s, and says: "All right! Check out this bad boy."

Describing his new computer with pride, he adds: "12 Megabytes of RAM. 500-megabyte hard drive. Built-in spreadsheet capabilities... And a modem that transmits at over 28,000 BPS."

Unimpressed, Phoebe comments asking: "What are you gonna use it for?"

Chandler looks a bit confused and replies saying: "Games and stuff..."

Let's decode what happened here:

The scene is turning into ridicule the fact that features are simply the characteristics of a proposition. Being proud of features doesn't make sense.

And this is what makes the scene funny: A mere list of feature misses the "so what?", which is what Phoebe is asking with a candid tone. "What are you gonna use it for?"

Features do not tell you what a proposition is for. They don't say anything about how people will use it and how it creates value for them.

Features are useful to build a proposition. But your audience will find the benefits to be more relevant.

Feature: Definition

"Roadmaps are evidence of strategy. Not a list of features."

– STEVE JOHNSON, Product management expert

Features help you describe your proposition at a technical level. They are all the characteristics and functionalities of your proposition.

Also called specs, features are especially useful in two situations:

1. Comparing propositions – By breaking down your proposition into individual features, you see how your proposition compares technically to alternatives.

2. Prioritising a product roadmap – Features are commonly used to describe elements of a product roadmap, which is the articulation of how your proposition could evolve over time.

When we think about features, the main challenge is to prioritise them. Should you add this feature to your proposition? If yes, when should you implement it?

- Should a chocolate brand wrap its chocolate bar in a biodegradable packaging?
- Should Microsoft Teams add the ability to hide your video on your screen without turning off your camera for the other participants?
- Should an e-commerce website implement the Facebook pixel that allows to track the performance of ads on Facebook and Instagram?

Developing new features comes at a cost. It's necessary to make sure that a new feature will create value for your audience and for your company too.

Prioritisation

There are three areas you need to look at when you are in the process of **prioritising** features:

1. **Desirability** is a marketing question. This is the focus of the Value Mix. Will the feature help your audience better achieve their goals? Will it fit with their beliefs? Is it something they will be willing to pay for?

2. **Feasibility** is a technical question. Can it be done? Is it legal? How long will it take to implement it? At what cost? These are questions for engineers, lawyers, industry experts, and tech partners.

3. **Viability** is a financial and strategic consideration. Your proposition has to be considered as a part of the overall business. Will it be profitable? Does it make sense for your organisation to do it? Is it aligned with your strategy? Adding a new feature creates additional costs (e.g., implementation cost and opportunity cost), so will it generate enough revenue to balance these costs?

Prioritisation looks like this Venn diagram:

Venn diagram for prioritising features

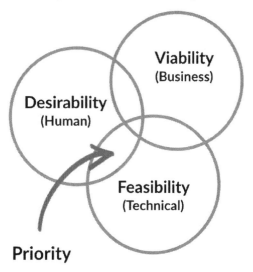

The prioritised features need to be desirable, viable, and feasible.

Key questions about your proposition:

What's the priority for your target audience? What are the must-haves? What is just nice to have?

Benefit: Definition

"People don't buy what you do; they buy how you make them feel."

— BERNADETTE JIWA, Branding expert

Benefits are the reasons (*logical and emotional*) that push your audience to buy your proposition. They tell your audience how your product or service creates value and what's in it for them.

A benefit is the outcome of a feature (or a set of features). You can use a simple formula to see how they relate to each other:

"A [*feature*], so that a [*benefit*]."

For example, the first iPod had [5GB] (*feature*), so that [you could have 1,000 songs your pocket] (*benefit*).

The benefit is the description of what a feature will mean to your audience:

- A laptop has a 10-inch screen, so that it's small and easy to carry around.
- A battery pack carries 5,200-mAh, so that you can fully charge your iPhone at least twice.

- A GoudronBlanc T-shirt is made with organic cotton, so that you can be proud of shopping more sustainably.

Having the right set of benefits will help to differentiate your proposition and make it stand out among the other alternatives.

A tool: The benefits ladder

Reframing features as benefits makes it easier for your audience to see how your proposition will improve their lives. But what could be difficult is to be relevant in the way you talk about each of the benefits.

The **benefits ladder** is a tool that helps you layer the emotional implication of a functional benefit. At the bottom, you get the feature. At the top, you get a series of emotional benefits.

To build a benefits ladder:

1. Pick a feature.
2. Think about what the feature means for the user. You must arrive at a quite functional benefit.
3. Repeat but this time using the benefit you just landed.
4. And then, repeat until you reach a benefit that seems too high level.

Most high-level benefits are about making people happier. What you need to find is the right level, i.e., a benefit that is emotional and tangible enough so it'll resonate with your audience.

Here's the example of a benefits ladder for an external phone charger:

The benefits ladder of an external charger

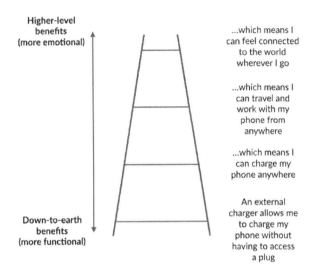

Higher-level benefits (more emotional)

...which means I can feel connected to the world wherever I go

...which means I can travel and work with my phone from anywhere

...which means I can charge my phone anywhere

Down-to-earth benefits (more functional)

An external charger allows me to charge my phone without having to access a plug

---

Key questions about your proposition:

What's in it for them? Why should they care about your proposition? How does your proposition help them achieve their goals?

Marketing question: Feature or Benefit?

You may have heard that your audience is more interested in the benefits than the features.

Indeed, benefits are the outcome of a feature (or set of features). They give your audience reasons to buy, since knowing the benefits tells them how your proposition can help them achieve their goals.

But sometimes, it's easier to talk about features to communicate how your proposition can help your audience.

It's the case when the audience is familiar with what a specific feature means for them.

- If I tell you "my iPhone has 8GB of memory", I can feel your compassion. Indeed, 8GB means that I am not able to store many photos, apps, and podcasts on my phone.

- If a store claims "open 24h", you know what it means. The store manager doesn't need to specify: "You can even come to our supermarket if you're running out of milk in the middle of the night."

- If you rent an "automatic" car, you know how it'll feel to drive it. There's no need to explain that you won't have to change gears and that the car does it automatically.

- If you buy 0% fat yogurt, you understand it'll be less heavy than the 5% fat version. You don't need to get it as "good to stay fit".

When the features are obvious, it can be more effective to let your audience make the jump to thinking about what it means for them rather than tell them about the benefits.

CHAPTER 9:

POSITIONING

It's not just about the soda

In 1985, The Coca-Cola Company introduced what is known as the "new Coke".

At the time, consumer preference for Coca-Cola was reported to be in decline. Blind tastes showed that Americans seemed to prefer the taste of Pepsi Cola. So The Coca-Cola Company decided to improve the formula of Coke. They replaced it with a formula called the "new Coke", which was chosen as the best alternative in taste tests by nearly 200,000 consumers.

But the launch of the new formula didn't go as expected. It led an unprecedented outcry in the US.

According to the Time, the company received over 40,000 letters of complaint and was flooded with phone calls and bad press. Three months later, they felt compelled to reintroduce the Coca-Cola "classic".

The Coca-Cola executives didn't expect that their target audience didn't want a better taste.

Indeed... Americans were buying a drink, but also a story.

They wanted the legend of the secret original formula, the symbol of their childhood, the pride of being American, and the most known brand in the world.

Positioning: Definition

"The most important decision is how to position your product."

— DAVID OGILVY, Founder of Ogilvy & Mather

Your **positioning strategy** is the set of stories you tell to differentiate your proposition and make it stand out against the available alternatives.

When you go to a Lidl, you experience the "we pass the savings to our customers" stories that Lidl stands for.

The storefront typically displays ads showing big discounts. In the shop, prices are surprisingly low. Most products are on shelves in their secondary packaging. The products are of good quality. And when you leave the store, you're offered a catalogue that features all the discounts that will be available the following week.

Everything is done to make the price-sensitive consumers feel that "it's like the same as in other supermarkets, but it's much cheaper".

Simply put, a positioning strategy creates a frame of reference that helps your audience understand what makes your proposition different and better *for* them.

It answers the question: "What is your proposition famous for?" And the answer must stick in people's minds.

Noticed vs. Unnoticed

"It's tricky to define better. But without a doubt, the heart and soul of a thriving enterprise is the irrational pursuit of becoming irresistible.

– SETH GODIN, Author of This Is Marketing

In a world where everything is one click away on Google, everyone wants to feel that they got the best and most relevant proposition.

You wouldn't like using a razor that is the second-best at making at a "baby butt smooth" shave. Or you wouldn't that your online shop is powered by the second-best e-commerce management system.

In today's world of unlimited choice and supply, getting noticed and standing out for being the most relevant alternative is critical. It's what will decide between the success or failure of your proposition.

You need a positioning strategy that makes your audience emotionally get how different your proposition is from the other alternatives and why it's so much better for them than the rest.

It shouldn't be the second-best. It should be seen as the best, and the most exciting and relevant option *for* them.

Positioning is perception

"Positioning is how you differentiate your brand in the mind. Positioning focuses on the perceptions of the prospect."

– Al Ries, Author of Positioning

The positioning of your proposition is based on **perception**, not facts. What matters is what *your audience* believes to be true, not what *you* think is true.

There's always a gap between what a customer thinks about a proposition and what the company wants them to think. Your positioning strategy isn't the same as your brand.

- Your positioning strategy is your attempt to influence your audience so that your proposition stands out in their eyes and is recognised as different, better, and more relevant than the other alternatives.
- Your brand isn't what you say it is. It's what your audience feels and believes about your proposition and the value it creates for them.

Positioning is about perception, but your positioning strategy has to be **authentic**. It isn't about lying. The stories you tell must be aligned with the customer experience you create.

Your audience needs a reason to believe your stories. This could be scientific evidence, product features, the founders' reputation, having famous customers, the company's heritage, what their friends are saying, celebrity endorsement, or any iconic element that supports your positioning strategy.

It's one thing to claim that your brand sells the most remarkable yoga clothes. It's another to claim it while showing that some of the most well-known yoga teachers use your products.

Positioning is about your audience

As I mentioned before, the image of your proposition depends on the perception of your audience. Your positioning strategy must be something *they* would find relevant and would like to believe.

- GoPro targets people who have a bias towards extreme sport and see themselves as adrenaline junkies.
- Red Bull focuses on people who believe that a beverage can help them go through the day and be better at what they do.
- Lidl appeals to consumers who tend to be more price-sensitive, and don't want to put a fortune in grocery shopping.
- Nespresso wants to be the choice of people who enjoy the taste of good coffee, but don't want to go through the hassle of becoming a barista at home.

The stories you tell must reinforce your audience's worldviews, but they should also position your proposition as being the most exciting and relevant in their context and to the goals they are trying to achieve.

These stories should alleviate their concern, and make your proposition stand out among the other available alternatives.

You must start seeing how the "audience" side of the Value Mix framework fits with the "proposition". Creating your positioning strategy requires to do a lot of research to understand your audience at a deeper level.

Positioning is putting things in boxes

As human beings, we tend to put things and people in boxes. It's our way of making sense of the world.

Boxes are patterns we've learnt to recognised based on our biases, beliefs, and experience of the world (*worldviews*). Putting things in boxes helps our brain know what to expect.

We do this with people. Who doesn't have a friend or family member who is considered as being "the funny one" or "the lazy one"?

But we also do the same with brands and propositions. Your positioning strategy isn't just a slogan or a logo. It's a system of stories and iconic elements that you use to help your audience put your proposition in the right box.

And not everyone shares the same worldviews. Different audiences will put your proposition in different boxes.

Android = cool phones that I can adapt to my needs and wants

iPhone = expensive phones

Audience A

iPhone = cool and beautiful phones that just work

Android = cheap and complicated phones

Audience B

One group of people see iPhones as expensive phones, while another group will believe that iPhones are cool and beautiful phones that just work. Inversely, Android phones can be considered as a symbol of technological freedom by one group and cheap and complicated by another group.

Positioning must be laser-focused

"I could have positioned Dove as a detergent bar for men with dirty hands, but chose instead to position it as a toilet bar for women with dry skin. This is still working 25 years later."

– DAVID OGILVY, Founder of Ogilvy & Mather

Defining the positioning of your proposition is about making choices. It requires to choose what you want your proposition to be famous for and to know to whom you should say, "yes, this is for you" and more importantly, "no, this proposition isn't for you".

Focus is at the heart of positioning. It's about identifying the one or two things that are the most relevant for your audience, that are easy to understand and remember, and that can be explained quickly to other people.

Your proposition can't be famous for too many things.

In 2017, Dropbox launched a software aimed for businesses called Paper. When the company launched

Paper, it described the software as "one part online document, one part collaboration, one part task management tool, one part content hub".

This is an example of a lack of focused positioning. If you search "dropbox paper review" on Google, you'll see how reviewers struggle to articulate what the software is for, whom it's for, and how it stands out among the other alternatives. The result? The makes it hard for the IT department of a company to explain to their colleagues why they should use it.

Positioning isn't just advertising

"The only thing that matters is everything."

– DAVID HIEATT, Founder of Hiut Denim Co

The positioning strategy for your proposition isn't just what you claim on an ad or a website. It's everything that shapes your proposition is perceived.

It's what the packaging looks like. It's how you make your audience feel when they buy and use your proposition. It's what they heard from their brother-in-law. It's what they see when they google the brand name. It's how your customer service team treats them. It's what influencers say about it.

It's also the iconic elements that stick in their minds when they think about your brand or your product category.

- It's the red sole of the Louboutin shoes.
- It's the orange boxes of Hermès.
- It's the bouncing lamp at the start of a Pixar movie.
- It's the no-frills seats of a Ryanair airplane.

- It's the shoes given to charity when you buy a pair of TOMS shoes.
- It's the way sales associates welcome you at the cashier of a Trader Joe's.
- It's your name on the cup you got at a Starbucks, even if it's sometimes misspelt.

Your positioning strategy is based on the stories you tell through copywriting, iconic elements, and customer experience. Your brand is how all of these make them feel.

Positioning helps you make decisions

"Everyone in the organisation should understand the brand positioning and use it as context for making decisions."

– DAVID OGILVY, Founder of Ogilvy & Mather

Your positioning strategy should be a North Star. It helps you and your team to make decisions about how to develop, sell, and improve your proposition. It's an organising framework that makes it easier to know what to do and what not to do.

When Apple decided to stand for "privacy", everyone in the organisation embraced the new positioning strategy.

The CEO talks publicly about privacy. The marketing team displayed the message "What happens on your iPhone, stays on your iPhone." on a massive advertising board in Las Vegas during the CES 2019. The product team implements features that protect privacy on your iPhone. The Intelligent Tracking Prevention of Safari stops advertisers from following you from site to site. Unlike other navigation apps, the Maps app doesn't keep a history of where you've been.

Every employee plays a role in making the positioning real and translating it into how customers perceive the proposition. Everyone from the CEO to the frontline should be aligned on the positioning strategy.

Key questions about your proposition:

What should your proposition be famous for? What do you want your audience to feel and believe? What do you want them to tell their friends?

CHAPTER 10:

CUSTOMER EXPERIENCE
+ USER EXPERIENCE

A perfect day to go to IKEA

Imagine... You're in your twenties and you're moving into an unfurnished flat (*context*).

Your reflex? "I should go to IKEA to get some stuff."

Now your challenge is to find how to get there. You need to find a friend who has a car or rent one to reach an Ikea store and bring back your purchase.

Once there, you go through an endless showroom. It feels like being in a museum. You choose the furniture you want. And, towards the end of the labyrinth, you pick up a few things for the kitchen. Then, you arrive in a warehouse where you have to find the furniture you selected. You put everything on a trolley. You pay and wonder whether you should get it delivered. But actually, it'll be more expensive and could take too much time. So you try to fit everything in your friend's car (*customer experience*).

Back home, you're facing your next challenge. You now have to understand the user manuals to build your own furniture. Once it's done, you're ready to invite your friends for dinner to show your newly furbished flat (*user experience*).

Though some elements may feel clunky, IKEA designed a perfect customer experience for what you wanted: getting affordable pieces of furniture that look good and do not empty your bank account (*goal and worldview*).

Customer Experience: Definition

"In the factory we make cosmetics; in the drugstore we sell hope."

— CHARLES REVSON, Co-founder of Revlon

Your **customer experience** (CX) is how your proposition shows up in the life of your audience.

All the interactions before and after purchasing your proposition are part of the customer experience. It goes from your ads to the shopping experience to the experience of using your proposition and talking about it with other users.

These are all the moments where you can delight your audience to build loyalty and encourage them to share their experience and recommend your proposition.

The customer experience isn't just about a product. It's how you create value and deliver it to your audience. It's how you make them feel. It's the embodiment of your positioning strategy.

Keep in mind that people do not buy a pile of features. They buy stories and experiences, which are designed to help them achieve the goals that arise in particular contexts, to reinforce their worldviews, and to alleviate their concerns, while doing all of these better and in more exciting and relevant ways than the other available alternatives.

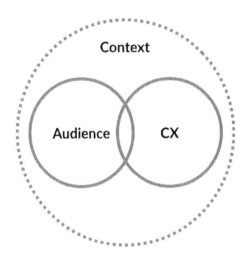

Make it remarkable

To keep running, a business must create a customer experience that consistently delivers at least what its customers expect to get, i.e., no bad surprises.

When you go to a coffee shop to grab a coffee with a friend, you expect a convenient location, good coffee, a clean space, and someone nice on the other side of the counter.

This the bare minimum for a coffee shop.

But this isn't what will push you to tell all your friends about this coffee shop. It just feels like any other coffee shop.

To be worth talking about, the customer experience must also create a little something that is **remarkable**. It should create something that makes you feel great and that is worth talking about.

Doing something slightly better than the other alternatives isn't enough to stand out. Think about it as two levels of customer experience:

1. **Good** is about creating enough value so that someone is going to try your proposition.
2. **Great** is about creating such a remarkable customer experience that someone who tried your proposition is going to tell their friends about it.

Being remarkable is about creating and delivering value beyond what's expected. It's about offering the most relevant alternative, but also the most exciting one.

Key questions about your proposition:

How will your proposition show up in the lives of your customers? What will make your customer experience remarkable? What will make it worth talking about?

User Experience: Definition

The **user experience** (UX) is the moment of consumption or use of your proposition.

It's a component of the customer experience. It's a key moment that will influence whether your user will come back to buy again, and whether they will recommend your proposition to others.

There's something to keep in mind. The user and the customer can be two different persons. A user doesn't always decide to buy the proposition. This is especially the case in two situations:

1. In B to B, the user of Microsoft Teams didn't decide to use it. This is the IT department that decided that all the employees of a company will have to use Teams for collaboration.

2. When someone receives a gift, they may or may not have decided on the gift. And for sure, they didn't pay for it. But this is why the user may have received a jumper that is too small or a toy that isn't exactly the Playmobil they wanted.

Though the idea of user experience comes from the tech world, it is also applicable to consumer goods. Think about the experience of using a notebook, having a chocolate bar, charging your electric car, or eating at a restaurant.

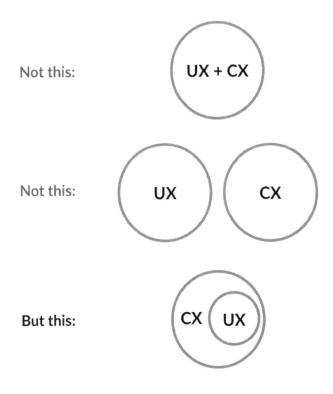

Not this: UX + CX

Not this: UX   CX

But this: CX UX

Evaluating the User Experience

To help you measure how relevant the user experience is, you can break it down into two attributes: "usefulness" and "usability".

1. **Usefulness** is about whether your proposition helps your audience achieve their goals. If a proposition is **not useful,** then, what's the point?

2. **Usability** is how easy and pleasant the user experience is for the user. If a proposition is **not easy to use,** the value your audience gets out it is limited by the friction created through the clunky user experience.

To stand out, the user experience needs one more thing. It needs "excitement".

3. **Excitement** is about providing a remarkable experience. It's making something happen that is worth talking about.

To create value for your audience, your proposition must be relevant, which requires both usefulness and usability. But it must also be exciting, making your audience feel great while using your proposition.

Key questions about your proposition:

How will they use your proposition? Will it be useful
and easy to use? How exciting will it be?

OVER TO YOU!

I wrote this at the beginning of the book:

"The Value Mix aims to make it easier for you to think about the nuances of creating products and services that people will want, i.e., creating value for them."

I really hope this book will help you to understand your audience at a deeper level and inspire you to find new ways to create value for them.

The ideal result would be if you end up launching a new proposition using the Value Mix.

Another great outcome would be if the framework helps you align with your team and partners when you run market research or work on creating new propositions.

The thinking that is at the foundation of the Value Mix has helped me create GoudronBlanc and delight thousands of customers around the world.

I honestly hope that this book will also help you build a stronger, better business that will find new ways to create value in our world.

Over to you, now!

Your Audience	Your Proposition
Worldviews	Customer Exp. / Positioning
Goals	+
Concerns	User Exp. / Features + Benefits
Context	Alternatives

ABOUT THE AUTHOR: GUERRIC

What I'm up to:

In 2011, I started GoudronBlanc, a brand for gentlemen who love wearing great T-shirts.

As I enjoy solving big challenges, I also work as an innovation consultant at ?What If! where I help Fortune 500 companies spot big business opportu-nities and create new meaningful propositions.

I have taught marketing and innovation at top business schools (incl. UCL, London Business School, Princeton, and Condé Nast College of Fashion & Design).

In 2018, I published The Value Mix, a book about creating new value propositions and released a new edition in 2021. I also recently published a second book called The Opportunity Lenses that focuses on spotting future business opportunities.

And I love helping people make cool stuff happen.

Find my latest reflections about strategy and innovation at Guerric.co.uk.

THE END.

The Value Mix is a short book. Short books are difficult to write. There's a lot of things to say, but only a few pages to say them.

But the challenge was worth it.

Nothing is more annoying for a reader than a book that was written to reach a certain minimum of pages. This is not a good demonstration of usability.

Many of my readers share this worldview. They want easy access to what matters most and some good stories along the way.

I'm sure you agree.

So I kept telling myself: "Make it exciting, useful, and easy to read."

Made in the USA
Las Vegas, NV
09 January 2022

40910858R00072